TINY
STITCHES

TINY STITCHES

BUTTONS, BADGES, PATCHES AND PINS TO EMBROIDER

İrem Yazici

Search Press

A QUARTO BOOK

First published in 2018 by
Search Press Ltd
Wellwood
North Farm Road
Kent TN2 3DR

ISBN:978-1-78221-711-4

10 9 8 7 6 5 4 3 2 1

Conceived, edited, and designed by
Quarto Publishing plc,
an imprint of The Quarto Group
6 Blundell Street
London N7 9BH

www.quartoknows.com
QUAR.304775

Senior editor: Kate Burkett
Senior art editor: Emma Clayton
Designers: Karin Skånberg and Abi Read
Illustrators: Charlotte Farmer and
Kuo Kang Chen
Photography: Phil Wilkins
Art director: Jess Hibbert
Publisher: Samantha Warrington

When working through this book, please use
either the metric or imperial measurement.

MIX
Paper from
responsible sources
FSC® C008047
www.fsc.org

CONTENTS

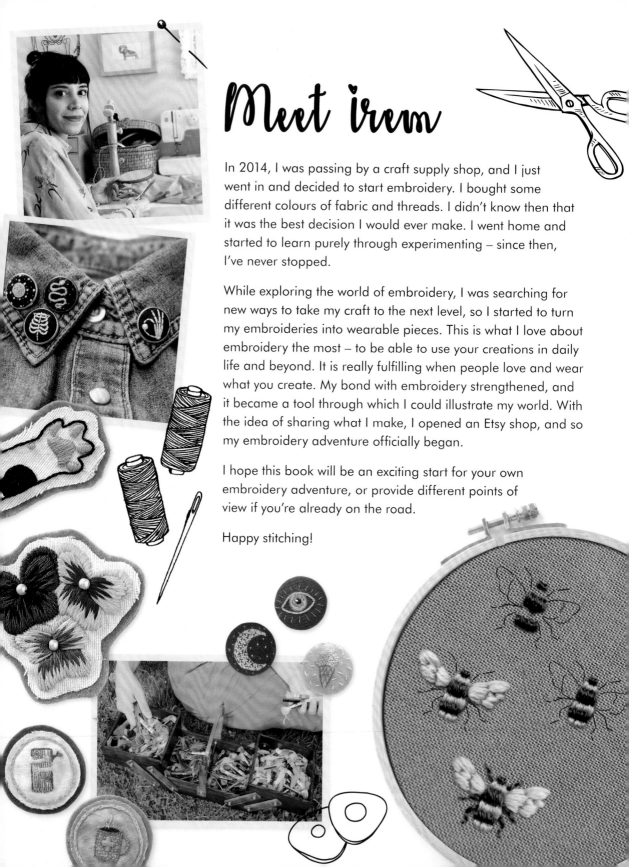

Meet İrem

In 2014, I was passing by a craft supply shop, and I just went in and decided to start embroidery. I bought some different colours of fabric and threads. I didn't know then that it was the best decision I would ever make. I went home and started to learn purely through experimenting – since then, I've never stopped.

While exploring the world of embroidery, I was searching for new ways to take my craft to the next level, so I started to turn my embroideries into wearable pieces. This is what I love about embroidery the most – to be able to use your creations in daily life and beyond. It is really fulfilling when people love and wear what you create. My bond with embroidery strengthened, and it became a tool through which I could illustrate my world. With the idea of sharing what I make, I opened an Etsy shop, and so my embroidery adventure officially began.

I hope this book will be an exciting start for your own embroidery adventure, or provide different points of view if you're already on the road.

Happy stitching!

Embroidery become a tool through which i could illustrate my world

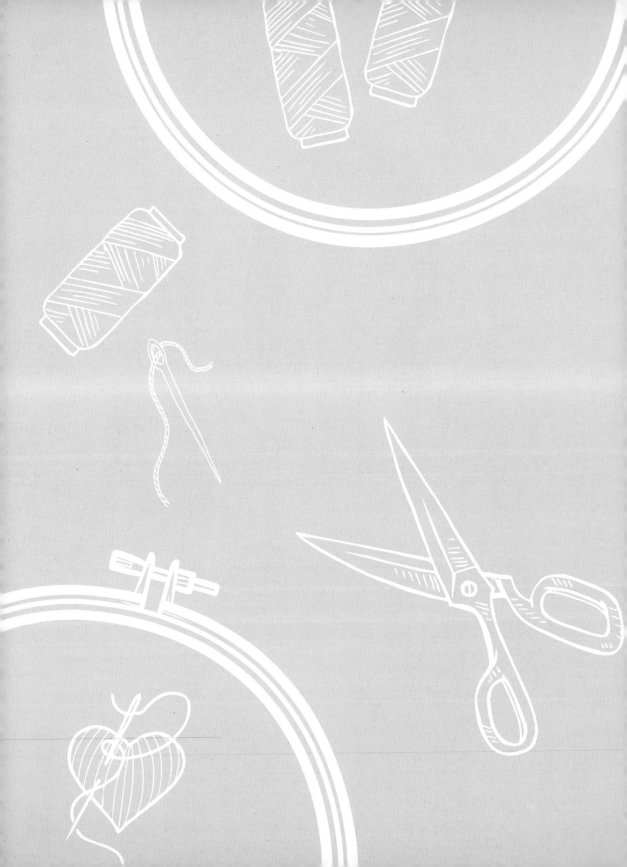

1

Embroidery 101

TOOLS AND MATERIALS

If you're an experienced stitcher, you probably have many tools and materials in your possession already. If you've never stitched before, don't worry, as you do not need all of these items to get started. You can make a perfect starter kit with a hoop, a scrap of fabric, embroidery needles, scissors and a few skeins of cotton thread.

THREAD

1 Cotton embroidery thread

The most common type of embroidery thread, cotton thread comes in a wide range of colours and can be used for most types of embroidery. Embroidery thread consists of six twisted strands that can be divided or combined to achieve a desired thickness.

2 Metallic thread

Metallic thread is used to enhance embroidery with a glittery effect. These threads can be delicate and difficult to handle, so it's best to work with shorter lengths.

FABRICS

As with thread, there are endless options when it comes to choosing which type of fabric to embroider on. Almost any fabric can be suitable for embroidery, but I tend to stick to woven and felt.

3 Woven

Woven fabrics cover a wide range and include any fabric made with horizontal and vertical threads. They are an excellent choice for embroidery because they keep their shape and are firm enough to support heavy stitches. Wovens come in an array of weights and types, ranging from lightweight muslin and quilter's cotton to medium linen and heavyweight canvas and duck cloth.

4 Felt

Felt is one of my favourite materials to work with because of its thickness and texture. It is available in a wide range of colours and thicknesses, and, unlike woven fabrics, will not fray along the cut edges. It can be made from natural fibres such as wool, synthetic fibres like rayon or acrylic, or a blend of both. I generally prefer 100% wool or wool-blended felt.

NEEDLES

Needles come in a variety of lengths and thicknesses, with different eyes and points, so select the type that suits the type of thread and fabric to be used. It's a good idea to keep a selection of needles to hand so that you can switch as needed. If you notice that you're having trouble pulling your thread through your fabric, opt for a larger needle. Or, if you notice your needle leaving large holes in your fabric, opt for one that's a bit finer.

5 Embroidery needles

Embroidery needles have a medium length with a long eye and a sharp point. They are useful for most general embroidery and are sized in reverse number order, so the higher the number, the finer the needle.

6 Chenille needles

Chenille needles are longer and thicker than embroidery needles, with a large eye and a sharp point. They are useful for thicker threads, yarn and ribbon.

7 Tapestry needles

Tapestry needles are similar to chenille needles, but with a blunt point. They are useful for fabrics that have a looser weave.

EMBROIDERY HOOPS

8 Embroidery hoop

An embroidery hoop holds your fabric taut as you stitch, which allows for even stitching and prevents puckering. I almost always use a hoop when stitching, except for when I stitch on felt and on ready-made garments with seams that might get in the way. Hoops come in a variety of sizes, given by their diameter. Whenever possible, choose one that can hold the entire design, so the hoop does not need to be shifted.

Embroidery hoop stand (optional)

This tool can be your hero if your embroidery adventure starts to get serious and you find yourself stitching for hours a day. It's not as portable as the other tools listed here, but when stitching at home it prevents the pain caused by holding a hoop for hours on end. Plus, it makes stitching French knots much easier as you're able to use both of your hands!

TRANSFER AND MARKING TOOLS

9 Lead pencils

Regular lead pencils are great to use for marking fabric. The marks they leave are light and, if not covered by your stitches, can be erased.

10 Chalk pencils

Chalk pencils are a good choice for marking on dark fabrics. Any uncovered marks can be brushed away easily once you've finished stitching.

11 Water-soluble pens

Water-soluble pens contain ink that disappears with water. Any marks that aren't fully covered with stitches can be removed with a damp cloth or cold-water rinse.

12 Air-soluble pens

Also called 'disappearing ink' pens, these pens contain ink that fades gradually.

Iron-on transfer sheets

Included in the envelope at the back of this book.

OTHER HELPFUL TOOLS

13 Scissors
14 Button-making kit
15 Tie tack pin setting

BASIC EMBROIDERY TECHNIQUES

ASSEMBLING AN EMBROIDERY HOOP

Hoops are necessary for all types of stitching where the fabric needs to be kept taut. They give better tension and help to prevent distortion, especially in linen and evenweave fabrics, which are softer than the aida fabrics. Keeping the fabric taut also helps make the finished stitching more even in appearance, and using a hoop reduces the amount of times the fabric is handled and crushed in the hand, which can leave marks from sweat, dirt and creases.

To assemble an embroidery hoop, adjust the screw of the outer ring so that it fits loosely over the inner ring. Place the inner ring on a flat surface.

Place the fabric over the inner ring, with the area to be worked in the centre.

Press the outer ring down over the fabric and inner ring, making sure the fabric is taut. Tighten the screw to secure the fabric.

TIP

Keep the fabric taut while you stitch by pulling on the edges of the fabric gently and evenly every so often, making sure you do not distort the design. If you find that your fabric is slipping excessively as you stitch, try wrapping the inner ring with cotton twill tape or add a layer of muslin. Stitch or glue the ends of the tape together in order to keep them secure.

HOW TO MAKE A PIN

Draw a circle that measures the same size as your tie tack pin setting, and cut it from the paper.

Remove your design from the hoop and cut around it, approximately 15 mm (½ in) away from the design.

Snip the edges of your fabric, leaving a 5 mm (⅕ in) space between each incision. To make sure you don't get too close to the design area, use the pointed tips of your scissors to make the incisions.

Glue each trimmed edge, then place your paper cabochon on the back of your design and fold all the trimmed and glued edges around it one by one, taking your time to make them neat. Wait for the fabric edge to stick to the paper before moving on to the next one.

Once you have stuck your fabric around the paper cabochon, glue inside your tie tack pin setting in preparation for placing the design. Starting from the edges, carefully place the design inside the setting. You can bend the cabochon a little to make it fit inside the setting. Push the edges carefully and slowly inside, using your fingertips.

HOW TO MAKE A BUTTON

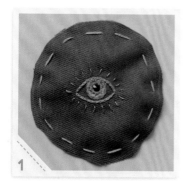

1

2

3

Using the transparent template in your button-making kit, trace a circle around your embroidered piece. Cut out your motif following the circle, then sew a line of running stitches inside the edge of the fabric.

Centre your button shell on the fabric circle. Using your fingers, gently push the shell down into the mould, then tuck the fabric into the button shell.

Cover the button shell with the button back.

4

5

Use the tool to firmly push the button back into place. When the back sits against the shell, you will hear a small clicking sound.

Remove your button by pressing on the mould.

HOW TO MAKE A PATCH

Remove the fabric from the hoop and carefully cut out the motif, approximately 5 mm (⅕ in) from the outline of the design.

Apply adhesive to the edges and middle of your design, using a foam brush or a small piece of sponge to spread it. This will prevent your fabric from fraying.

Place the motif, with the glued side facing down, onto the piece of felt. Press firmly in place and wipe away any excess glue.

Once the adhesive has dried, carefully cut the design from the felt, leaving a 5 mm (⅕ in) border around the edge.

HOW TO MAKE A BADGE

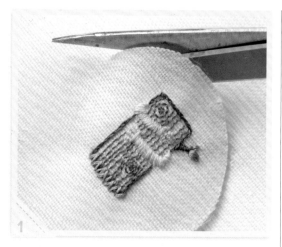

Draw a circle measuring 43 mm (½ in) in diameter around your motif. Remove the fabric from the hoop and cut out the motif, allowing approximately a 5 mm (⅕ in) allowance from the circle you drew.

Assemble the felt sheet in your hoop and place the motif on top. Stitch your fabric onto the felt using split stitch and six strands of any colour thread, following the circle line you drew in Step 1.

Carefully cut out the design from the felt, leaving a 5 mm (⅕ in) border around the edge.

Stitch to your chosen garment.

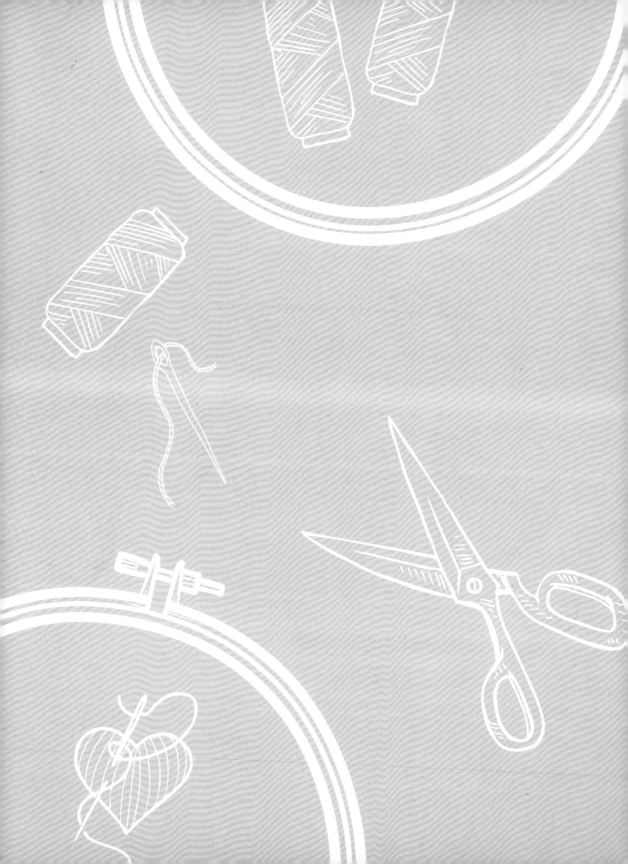

2

Tiny Hoops

A NIGHT IN THE FOREST

TEMPLATE *Page* 122 REFERENCE

Embrace the call of the wild with this beautiful forest scene mini hoop. Just grab some marshmallows to toast for that authentic campfire feeling. . .

TOOLS AND MATERIALS

· Transfer and marking tools
· Dark blue or black fabric
· 8 cm (3 in) hoop
· Needle
· Scissors

THREAD COLOURS USED

· Light jade, 2 strands
· Celadon green, 2 strands
· Dark blue green, 2 strands
· Olive green, 4 strands
· Medium olive green, 4 strands
· Apricot, 3 strands
· Light straw, 2 strands
· Light brown, 3 strands
· Light khaki green, 3 strands
· Light yellow beige, 3 strands
· Precious metals dark gold, 2 strands

STITCHES USED

· Satin stitch
· Straight stitch
· French knots
· Stem stitch

THE PROCESS

Transfer the forest motif (see Templates, page 122, or, alternatively, you can use the iron-on transfer paper at the back of the book) onto the piece of fabric, then place into an embroidery hoop (see page 12).

Beginning with the pine tree, start at the top level and work in satin stitch using two strands of light jade, then continue in the same colour for the next two lower levels of the tree.

Continuing in satin stitch, for the three middle levels of the tree use two strands of celadon green, and for the bottom levels use two strands of dark blue green. Repeat Steps 1 and 2 to make the second pine tree.

For the lower part of the apple tree, fill the area using tiny, short straight stitches worked in four strands of olive green. They should look like confetti, but keep them touching each other and placed irregularly.

For the top of the apple tree, continue working tiny, short straight stitches in four strands of medium olive green. Repeat Steps 3 and 4 to make the second apple tree. Then make the fruits for the apple tree using French knots. Work in two strands of apricot for the left tree and two strands of light straw for the right.

For the tree in the middle, use three strands of light brown and stitch its body with a single, long straight stitch. Then work its branches in the same way. Add its leaves by working tiny, short straight stitches using three strands of light khaki green around each branch.

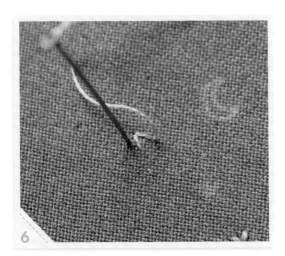

Make the stars using straight stitches worked in one strand of light yellow beige, as if you were drawing a star on a notebook.

Use one strand of apricot to make the tail of the shooting star, worked from two long straight stitches. Use two strands of light yellow beige to make tiny, short straight stitches for the twinkling dots. Finally, stitch the moon using two strands of precious metals dark gold and stem stitch. Work the outline first, then fill the inside using the same stitch.

DESERT LANDSCAPE

TEMPLATE *Page* REFERENCE 122

Not all deserts are made of endless sand dunes, as this beautiful landscape shows. Grab your water bottle, pull on your walking boots and prepare to take a trip into the great outdoors.

TOOLS AND MATERIALS

- Transfer and marking tools
- Blue fabric
- 8 cm (3 in) hoop
- Needle
- Scissors

THREAD COLOURS USED

- Dark blue green, 3 strands
- Celadon green, 3 strands
- Light jade, 3 strands
- Very dark olive green, 6 strands
- Dark old gold, 2 strands
- Medium golden olive, 3 strands
- Light golden olive, 6 strands
- Tan, 3 strands
- Medium gold, 3 strands
- Light plum, 2 strands
- Medium lavender, 4 strands
- Light Nile green, 2 strands
- Medium jade, 1 strand
- Medium apricot, 1 strand
- Apricot, 1 strand
- Very dark desert sand, 3 strands
- Desert sand, 3 strands
- Ultra very light terracotta, 3 strands
- Medium light moss green, 2 strands
- Light lemon, 2 strands

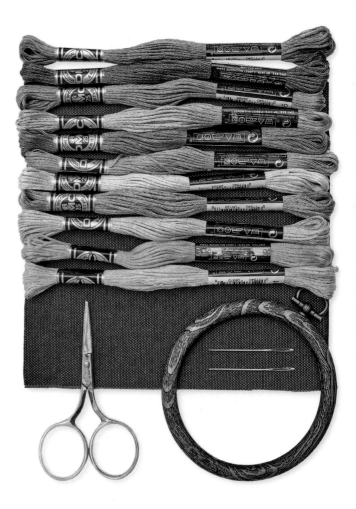

STITCHES USED

- Satin stitch
- Split stitch
- Straight stitch
- French knots

THE PROCESS

Transfer the desert motif (see Templates, page 122, or, alternatively, you can use the iron-on transfer paper at the back of the book) onto the piece of fabric, then place into an embroidery hoop (see page 12).

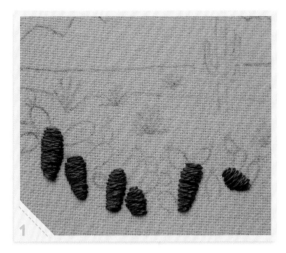

Start with the bunny ear cacti and stitch all the lower sections using three strands of dark blue green and satin stitch.

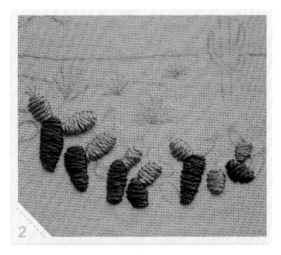

Work the middle sections using three strands of celadon green and satin stitch.

Finally, stitch the upper sections using three strands of light jade and satin stitch.

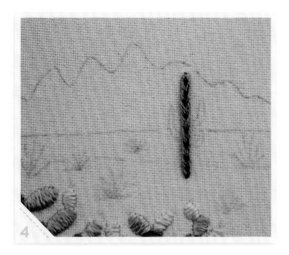

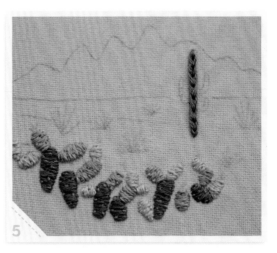

For the cactus in the middle of the desert, work its body in split stitch using six strands of very dark olive green.

Now add dots to the bunny ear cacti. Use two strands of dark old gold to make tiny straight stitches on top of the green satin-stitched layers.

Add branches to the tall cactus using split stitch once again. Use three strands of medium golden olive for the left and bottom right branch, and three strands of light golden olive for the upper right branch.

Now it's time to work on the ground. For the first part, use three strands of tan and make small, short straight stitches like tiny seeds or confetti. They should look like pebbles on the ground, so just go freestyle and keep them irregular.

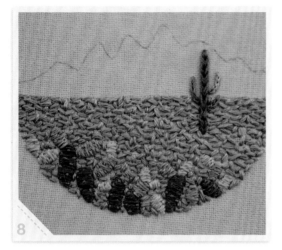

After stitching the first part of the ground, continue in the same style, using three strands of medium gold for the middle part, and three strands of light golden olive for the upper part.

Once the ground is finished, it's time to add the flowers to the bunny ear cacti. Stitch them using two strands of light plum, making tiny, short straight stitches (like seeds) on the upper section of each cactus.

Next, we're going to add the tiny succulents on the ground. Because the ground was stitched first, the outlines of the succulents are now invisible, so we're going to spot their places by referring to the design on the transfer paper and then make the stitches accordingly. For the lilac succulents, work straight stitches using four strands of medium lavender. For the pale green aloe veras, work straight stitches using two strands of light Nile green.

For the red flowers, work their leaves in straight stitch using one strand of medium jade, then make tiny French knots at the end of each leaf using one strand of medium apricot for the plant on the left, and one strand of apricot for the plant on the right. Work the first level of the mountains in straight stitch using three strands of very dark desert sand. Make long, horizontal straight stitches to fill the first level; they don't need to be equal sizes, so feel free to go with what you think looks good.

Following the same technique, stitch the rest of the mountains using three strands of desert sand for the second level, and three strands of ultra very light terracotta for the third level.

Add some shading to the large cactus using two strands of medium light moss green and split stitch. Work long stitches down the left side of the cactus's body and a small row of split stitches along the top of the top right branch, following the curve.

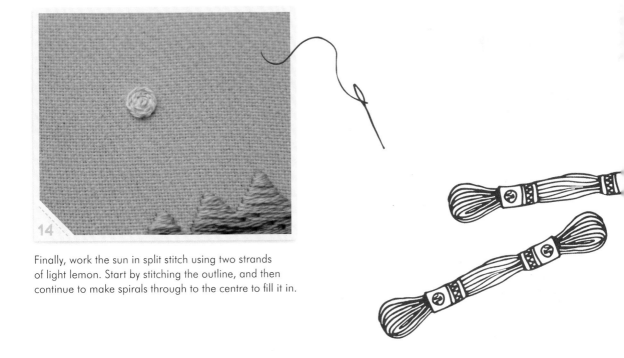

Finally, work the sun in split stitch using two strands of light lemon. Start by stitching the outline, and then continue to make spirals through to the centre to fill it in.

SUMMER SUNSET

This beautiful tropical sunset is just what you need to help you relax at the end of a long day. Close your eyes and you can almost hear the waves lapping at the shore. . .

TEMPLATE
Page
119
REFERENCE

TOOLS AND MATERIALS

- Transfer and marking tools
- Honey or mustard fabric
- 8 cm (3 in) hoop
- Needle
- Scissors

THREAD COLOURS USED

- Very dark turquoise, 3 strands
- Nile green, 2 strands
- Light mauve, 6 strands
- Medium apricot, 5 strands
- Bright orange red, 3 strands
- Light old gold, 3 strands
- White, 3 strands
- Very dark old gold, 6 strands
- Medium green grey, 4 strands
- Dark green grey, 4 strands
- Dark antique blue, 4 strands
- Very dark beaver grey, 1 strand
- Medium golden olive, 2 strands
- Apricot, 4 strands
- Light yellow beige, 1 strand

STITCHES USED

- Satin stitch
- Straight stitch
- Seed stitch
- French knots
- Brick stitch
- Split stitch
- Stem stitch

THE PROCESS

Transfer the beach motif (see Templates, page 119, or, alternatively, you can use the iron-on transfer paper at the back of the book) onto the piece of fabric, then place into an embroidery hoop (see page 12).

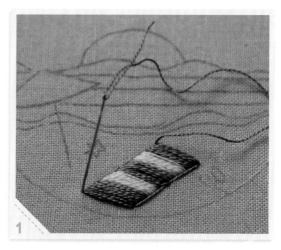

Let's start with the towel on the sand. Stitch the dark blue parts using two strands of very dark turquoise, and the light blue parts using two strands of Nile green, both in satin stitch. Make sure the stitches are going in the same direction as the towel's stripes. Once you have finished the satin stitching, outline the right and the left edges of the towel using one strand of very dark turquoise to make a single straight stitch on each side.

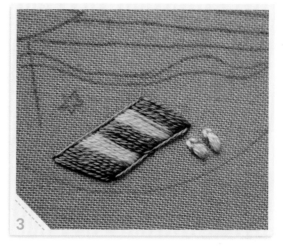

For the flip-flops, make two short seed stitches for each using six strands of light mauve.

Using four strands of medium apricot, work single, tiny straight stitches on the stitched area to make the thongs.

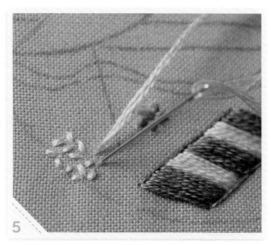

Stitch the starfish on the shore using three strands of bright orange red, making tiny, short seed stitches for each arm. Work each of the stitches from the upper outside edge into the centre.

Stitch the sand using three strands of light old gold, making small, confetti-like straight stitches. Start by making three tiny, short straight stitches that form a triangle, without the ends touching. Repeat this pattern to fill the whole area, keeping the stitches at roughly the same size.

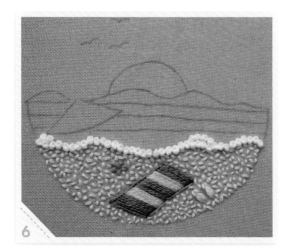

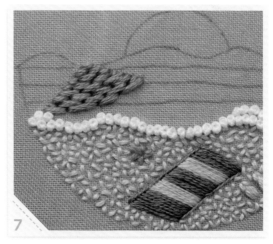

Stitch the sea foam using three strands of white to work a row of French knots.

For the straw parasol, use six strands of very dark old gold and work in brick stitch, following the horizontal direction of the parasol.

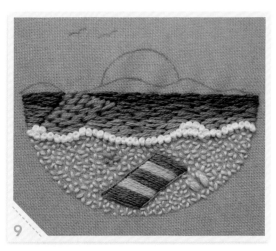

For the sea, start with the first level and use four strands of medium green grey to make horizontal long and short stitches in irregular sizes. It's like making a brick stitch but in more of a free form.

Repeat Step 8 to stitch the second and the third levels of the sea using four strands of dark green grey for the second level, and four strands of dark antique blue for the third level.

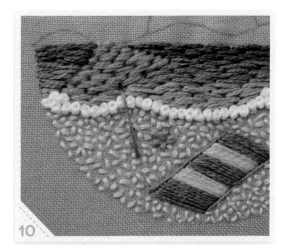

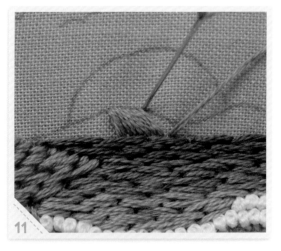

Once the sea is finished, we can add the base of the parasol. To make the base, first spot its position, then use one strand of very dark beaver grey to work three single straight stitches from the edge of the parasol to the sand.

For the mountains, use two strands of medium golden olive and satin stitch, making sure you stitch each part of the mountain in a different direction. For example, stitch the first part in a northwesterly direction, then stitch the next part in a northeasterly direction, and continue to follow that order. Make sure you start your stitches at the top edge of the mountains and end at the sea line.

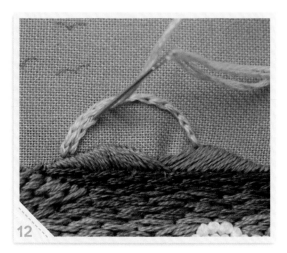

To make the sun, work four strands of apricot in split stitch. Start with stitching the outline, then continue working inwards towards the centre, as shown.

To finish, neaten the outside edge of the sun using one strand of medium apricot to work a line of stem stitch.

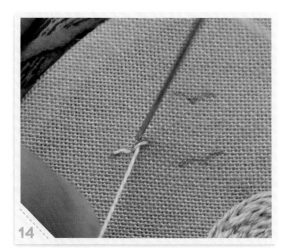

Use one strand of light yellow beige to stitch the flying birds in the sky. For every bird, make a single straight stitch starting from the right/left point of its wing to the centre of the bird (where its head would be), leave a little loop of thread on the surface of the fabric and then bring your needle up in the middle of the wing and down at a point above the wing. Repeat this for all the birds.

3

Precious Pins

PINEAPPLE PARADISE

TEMPLATE
Page
119
REFERENCE

Tutti frutti! Add a touch of fantastic tropical chic to your everyday outfits with this cute pineapple pin, and take the sunshine with you wherever you go. . .

TOOLS AND MATERIALS

- Transfer and marking tools
- Blue fabric
- Hoop
- Needle
- Scissors
- Cabochon paper (300 g / 11 oz)
- Tie tack pin setting
- Glue

THREAD COLOURS USED

- Medium mustard, 2 strands
- Light brown, 1 strand
- Very dark jade, 2 strands
- Medium jade, 2 strands

STITCHES USED

- Split stitch
- French knots
- Straight stitch
- Stem stitch

Transfer the pineapple motif (see Templates, page 119, or, alternatively, you can use the iron-on transfer paper at the back of the book) onto the piece of fabric, then place into an embroidery hoop (see page 12). Start with the body of the pineapple. First work its outline in split stitch using two strands of medium mustard, then continue, working in rounds towards the centre.

Work the dots on the pineapple using one strand of light brown to make French knots.

For the leaves, start with the middle leaf and make a single straight stitch using two strands of very dark jade. Use two strands of medium jade for the next leaves on the left and right, and outline them in stem stitch. Continue in this colour order until all leaves are stitched.

THE BEE'S KNEES

Set your creativity buzzing with this wildlife-inspired pin.
With its cheery colours and delicate design, this little
bumblebee looks cute on cuffs and collars as well. . .

TEMPLATE
Page
119
REFERENCE

TOOLS AND MATERIALS

· Transfer and marking tools
· Mustard or orange fabric
· Hoop
· Needle
· Scissors
· Cabochon paper (300 g / 11 oz)
· Tie tack pin setting
· Glue

THREAD COLOURS USED

· Ultra dark beaver grey, 3 strands
· Topaz, 2 strands
· Light yellow beige, 3 strands

STITCHES USED

· Satin stitch
· Straight stitch

THE PROCESS

Transfer the bumblebee motif (see Templates, page 119, or, alternatively, you can use the iron-on transfer paper at the back of the book) onto the piece of fabric, then place into an embroidery hoop (see page 12).

1 With two strands of ultra dark beaver grey, stitch the head using satin stitch. Continue stitching the body in the same way, leaving a gap between the head, middle and lower body.

2 With satin stitch, finish the body using two strands of topaz to fill the gaps.

3 Create the wings using straight stitch in three strands of light yellow beige.

4 For the legs, work small straight stitches using one strand of ultra dark beaver grey.

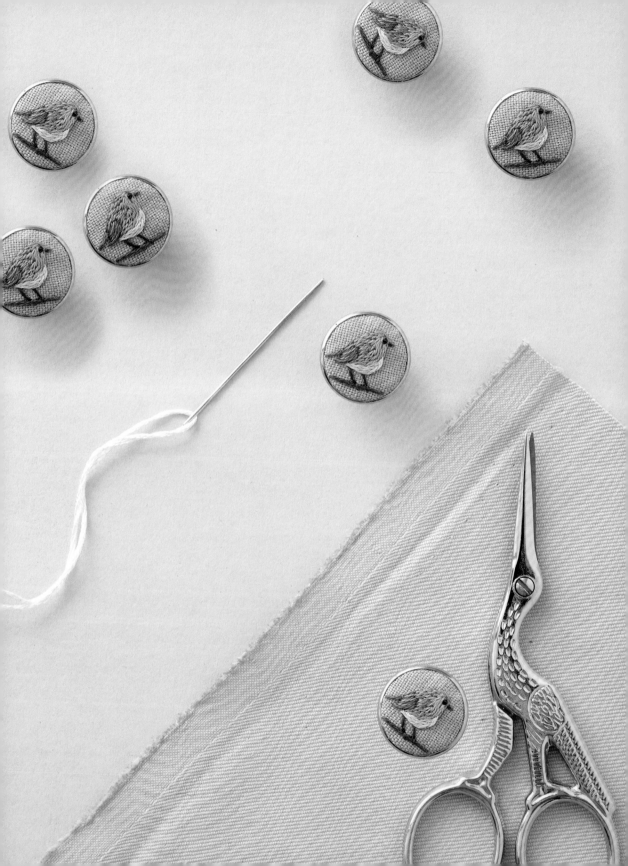

ROCKIN' ROBIN

TEMPLATE *Page* 121 REFERENCE

This cheerful little bird can always be easily identified by its distinctive red breast as it hops around gardens and tweets a happy song.

TOOLS AND MATERIALS

- Transfer and marking tools
- Lilac fabric
- Hoop
- Needle
- Scissors
- Cabochon paper (300 g / 11 oz)
- Tie tack pin setting
- Glue

THREAD COLOURS USED

- Light orange spice, 1 strand
- Medium mocha brown, 2 strands
- Drab brown, 4 strands
- Mocha brown, 2 strands
- Ecru, 1 strand
- Black, 2 strands
- Ultra dark beaver grey, 2 strands
- Dark golden olive, 1 strand

STITCHES USED

- Straight stitch
- Satin stitch

THE PROCESS

Transfer the robin motif (see Templates, page 121, or, alternatively, you can use the iron-on transfer paper at the back of the book) onto the piece of fabric, and place into an embroidery hoop (see page 12).

Start with the orange area, where the eye of the bird is positioned, and fill the space with long and short straight stitches using one strand of light orange spice. Make sure that your stitches follow the direction of the shape of the bird's body, in a roughly southwesterly direction. Your stitches don't have to be the same size here and can be freestyle.

Next, start to stitch the top of the head using one strand of medium mocha brown. Again, make freestyle long and short straight stitches, following the direction of the head.

For the wing, use two strands of drab brown and fill the area with satin stitch, following the direction of the wing. Work one long straight stitch for the tail using two strands of drab brown, and then make a few lines on the wing using straight stitches and one strand of medium mocha brown.

Stitch the belly area using one strand of mocha brown and one strand of ecru. Once again, use a freestyle combination of long and short straight stitches, following the direction of the belly.

For the eye, make a tiny, short straight stitch using two strands of black, and then use one strand of ultra dark beaver grey to make the beak with another tiny, short straight stitch.

Make the branch by working two long straight stitches using one strand of dark golden olive. Work the legs in straight stitches using one strand of ultra dark beaver grey, and stitch the feet as a second layer on top of the branch.

POPPY

TEMPLATE
Page
119
REFERENCE

These beautiful, dainty flowers can often be found growing wild in hedgerows and are a sure sign that summer is on its way.

TOOLS AND MATERIALS

- Transfer and marking tools
- Pink fabric
- Hoop
- Needle
- Scissors
- Cabochon paper (300 g / 11 oz)
- Tie tack pin setting
- Glue

THREAD COLOURS USED

- Bright orange red, 4 strands
- Bright orange, 2 strands
- Medium apricot, 4 strands
- Dark brown grey, 4 strands
- White, 3 strands
- Medium golden olive, 1 strand
- Golden olive, 1 strand
- Dark topaz, 3 strands

STITCHES USED

- Satin stitch
- French knots
- Stem stitch
- Seed stitch

THE PROCESS

Transfer the poppy motif (see Templates, page 119, or, alternatively, you can use the iron-on transfer paper at the back of the book) onto the piece of fabric, then place into an embroidery hoop (see page 12).

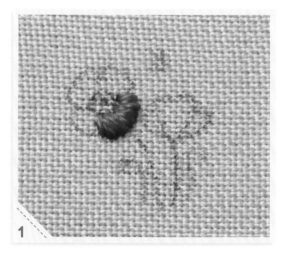

Let's start with the poppy on the left. It has four petals, and we're going to stitch its bottom petal first using two strands of bright orange red and satin stitch. Make sure your stitches go from the edge of the petal to the centre of the flower.

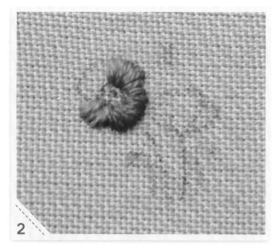

For the petals on the left and right, work them in satin stitch using two strands of bright orange, once again making sure that you take your stitches from the outside edges to the centre.

For the upper petal, use two strands of medium apricot and satin stitch, working your stitches from the outside in once again.

Fill in the middle of the poppy with French knots using one strand of dark brown grey. Finish by making a single French knot in the centre using one strand of white.

For the poppy on the right, work the middle petal first using two strands of bright orange red and satin stitch, stitching from the upper edge of the petal to its stem. Use two strands of medium apricot for the petals on the left and right, and stitch them in the same way.

Use one strand of medium golden olive to work the stems of the poppies using stem stitch. For the buds, use one strand of golden olive to stitch the stem (in stem stitch), and make the bud parts by working tiny seed stitches.

Stitch the bee by making tiny seed stitches using three strands of dark topaz for the dark parts, and three strands of dark brown grey for the black part in the middle. Add the wings by making a single tiny seed stitch for each wing using two strands of white.

PLANET SATURN

TEMPLATE Page 119 REFERENCE

As the second largest planet in our Solar System, Saturn and its distinctive rings are definitely worth commemorating. Launch your stitching skills into orbit with this funky pin that is almost out of this world.

TOOLS AND MATERIALS

- Transfer and marking tools
- Black fabric
- Hoop
- Needle
- Scissors
- Cabochon paper (300 g / 11 oz)
- Tie tack pin setting
- Glue

THREAD COLOURS USED

- Pale pumpkin, 2 strands
- Light plum, 3 strands
- Precious metals dark gold, 2 strands

STITCHES USED

- Split stitch
- Stem stitch
- Straight stitch

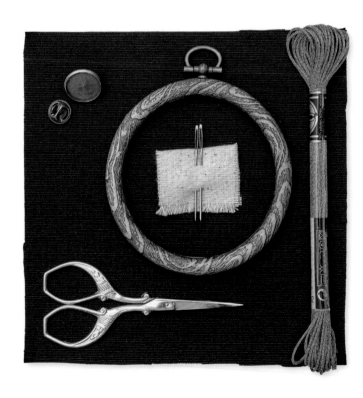

THE PROCESS

Transfer the Saturn motif (see Templates, page 119, or, alternatively, you can use the iron-on transfer paper at the back of the book) onto the piece of fabric, then place into an embroidery hoop (see page 12).

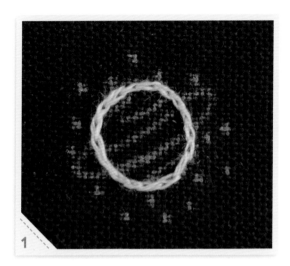

Start by working the outline of the planet in split stitch using two strands of pale pumpkin.

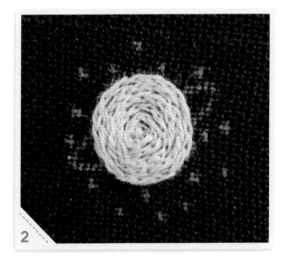

Continue in split stitch and work decreasingly smaller loops into the centre of the planet.

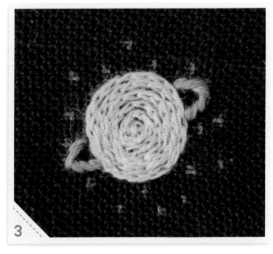

To make the ring, begin by working the parts on the left and on the right in stem stitch using three strands of light plum.

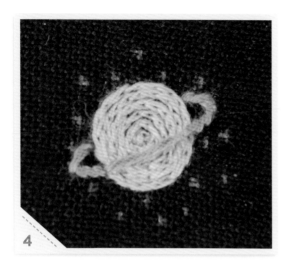

To complete the ring, make a single straight stitch across the planet, from right to left.

Finally, make the surrounding stars by working tiny straight stitches in two strands of precious metals dark gold.

Beautiful Buttons

THE ALL-SEEING EYE

TEMPLATE *Page* 124 REFERENCE

For centuries, eyes have been fascinating objects, and they can symbolise many different things in different cultures, from clairvoyance to wisdom and good luck. And even better, they are the perfect size for a button project.

TOOLS AND MATERIALS

· Transfer and marking tools
· Dark blue or green fabric
· Hoop
· Needle
· Scissors
· Button-making kit

THREAD COLOURS USED

· Black, 2 strands
· White, 3 strands
· Dark gold, 3 strands
· Light golden olive, 3 strands
· Light brown, 1 strand
· Medium apricot, 3 strands
· Apricot, 2 strands
· Precious metals dark gold,
  1 strand

STITCHES USED

· Satin stitch
· Straight stitch
· Split stitch

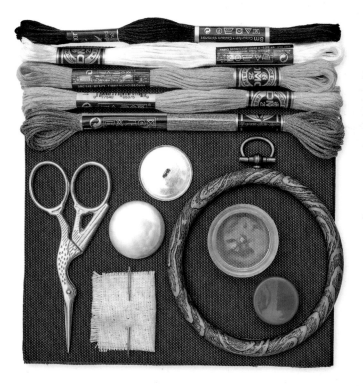

THE PROCESS

Transfer the eye motif (see Templates, page 124, or, alternatively, you can use the iron-on transfer paper at the back of the book) onto the piece of fabric, then place into an embroidery hoop (see page 12).

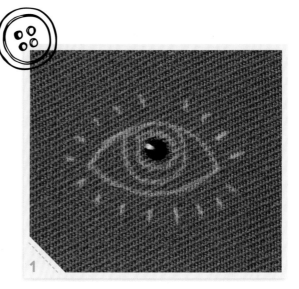

Start with the pupil of the eye using two strands of black and satin stitch. To create the light effect on the pupil, use three strands of white to work a couple of small straight stitches.

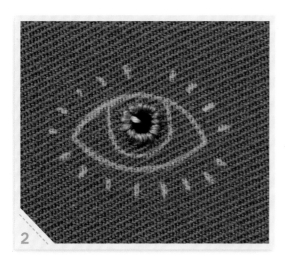

Fill the first part of the iris using satin stitch, worked in three strands of dark gold. Work the stitches from the outside edge in towards the pupil.

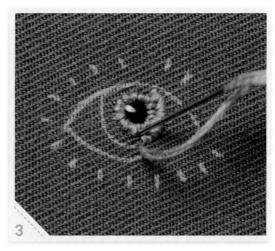

Continue in satin stitch for the second part of the iris, this time using three strands of light golden olive. Once again, work the stitches from the outer edge inwards.

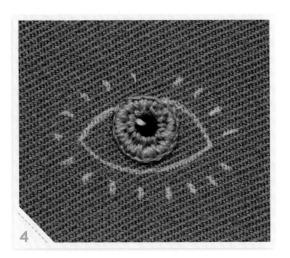

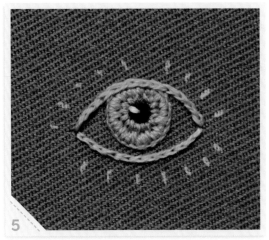

Outline the iris in split stitch using one strand of light brown.

Work the top outline of the eye in split stitch using three strands of medium apricot. Then stitch the bottom outline of the eye in split stitch using two strands of apricot.

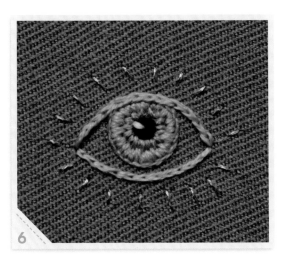

For the sparkles, use one strand of precious metals dark gold to make short straight stitches.

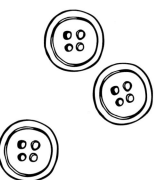

LIKE A MOTH TO A FLAME

TEMPLATE
Page
120
REFERENCE

Capture the delicate beauty of the moth in this dainty button.
With so many varieties to take inspiration from, you can easily
customise the colours and design to your own taste.

TOOLS AND MATERIALS

- Transfer and marking tools
- White or ecru fabric
- Hoop
- Needle
- Scissors
- Button-making kit

THREAD COLOURS USED

- Very dark golden olive, 2 strands
- Very light apricot, 2 strands
- Light jade, 3 strands
- Light olive green, 4 strands
- Light lemon, 6 strands
- Apricot, 4 strands
- Black, 1 strand

STITCHES USED

- Satin stitch
- French knots
- Straight stitch
- Stem stitch
- Back stitch

THE PROCESS

Transfer the moth motif (see Templates, page 120, or, alternatively, you can use the iron-on transfer paper at the back of the book) onto the piece of fabric, then place into an embroidery hoop (see page 12).

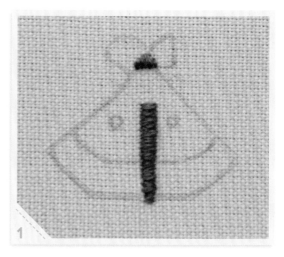

Start by working the head in satin stitch using two strands of very dark golden olive. Continue in the same colour and stitch to make the body, as shown.

Fill inside the neck area by working a cluster of French knots using two strands of very light apricot.

Next, work the upper parts of both wings in long and short straight stitches using three strands of light jade.

Work the lower parts of the wings in satin stitch using four strands of light olive green.

For decoration, make one French knot in the middle of each wing using six strands of light lemon.

To make the tiny dots on the lower part of the wings, work tiny straight stitches along the bottom of each wing using three strands of apricot.

Outline the bottom edge of both wings using stem stitch and one strand of apricot, then add the antennae and legs in back stitch using one strand of black.

PRICKLY CACTUS

If you love all things green and prickly, then this is the perfect project for you. Feed your cactus obsession with this cute button, and wear your heart, or rather, your cactus, on your sleeve for all to see.

TEMPLATE
Page
124
REFERENCE

TOOLS AND MATERIALS

- Transfer and marking tools
- Pink fabric
- Hoop
- Needle
- Scissors
- Button-making kit

THREAD COLOURS USED

- Celadon green, 2 strands
- Light straw, 3 strands
- Medium apricot, 3 strands
- Dark topaz, 3 strands

STITCHES USED

- Split stitch
- Straight stitch
- Seed stitch
- French knots

THE PROCESS

Transfer the cactus motif (see Templates, page 124, or, alternatively, you can use the iron-on transfer paper at the back of the book) onto the piece of fabric, then place into an embroidery hoop (see page 12).

1 Start with the bottom section of the cactus using two strands of celadon green and split stitch. First work the outline, then continue working rounds to fill it in. Stitch the other sections in the same way.

2 To make the dots on the cactus, use three strands of light straw and make tiny, very short straight stitches on the stitched background.

3 Add the flowers to the cactus using three strands of medium apricot to work tiny, short seed stitches.

4 Finish off by stitching the ground using three strands of dark topaz to make a row of French knots.

ICE-CREAM CONE

TEMPLATE
Page
120
REFERENCE

I scream, you scream, we all scream for ice cream. . . Add this cute button to your bag or top, and enjoy a sweet treat wherever you go. Why not change the colours to make your favourite flavours. . . ?

TOOLS AND MATERIALS

- Transfer and marking tools
- Lilac fabric
- Hoop
- Needle
- Scissors
- Button-making kit

THREAD COLOURS USED

- Apricot, 1 strand
- Light sea green, 1 strand
- Light straw, 2 strands
- Medium gold, 3 strands
- Light brown, 2 strands
- Light Nile green, 2 strands

STITCHES USED

- French knots
- Seed stitch
- Split stitch
- Satin stitch
- Straight stitch

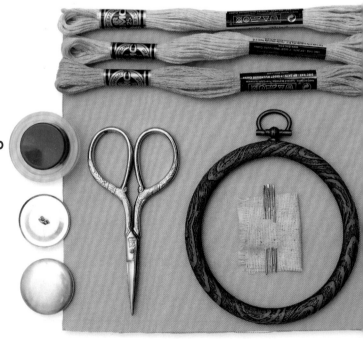

THE PROCESS

Transfer the ice cream motif (see Templates, page 120, or, alternatively, you can use the iron-on transfer paper at the back of the book) onto the piece of fabric, then place into an embroidery hoop (see page 12).

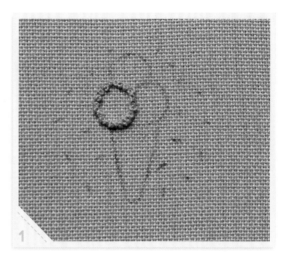

Start with the ball on the left. Work the outline in French knots using one strand of apricot. Then fill the rest of the ball using French knots in the same colour.

Fill the ball on the right with irregular tiny seed stitches using one strand of light sea green. They should look like confetti but more continuous.

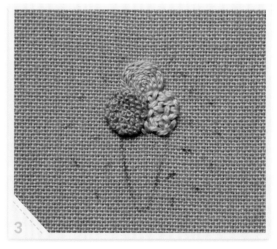

For the top ball, first make the outline using two strands of light straw and split stitch. Continue circling inwards using split stitch to fill the ball.

Use three strands of medium gold to work the cone in satin stitch.

Make straight stitches parallel to the edges of the cone using one strand of light brown. To create the cornet pattern, make stitches parallel to the right edge, then make stitches parallel to the left edge (they should make crosses). Once you have created the cornet pattern, outline the edge in straight stitch using one strand of light brown.

Finally, add the sprinkles using two strands of light Nile green to make short seed stitches all around.

OVER THE FLORAL MOON

TEMPLATE
Page
124
REFERENCE

This pretty crescent moon combines the current trends of astronomical symbols and all-things floral in one striking pattern that looks great on jewellery and accessories, as well as buttons.

TOOLS AND MATERIALS

· Transfer and marking tools
· Black fabric
· Hoop
· Needle
· Scissors
· Button-making kit

THREAD COLOURS USED

· Medium old gold, 3 strands
· Light old gold, 3 strands
· Precious metals dark gold, 3 strands

STITCHES USED

· Back stitch
· Seed stitch
· French knots
· Straight stitch

THE PROCESS

Transfer the moon motif (see Templates, page 124, or, alternatively, you can use the iron-on transfer paper at the back of the book) onto the piece of fabric, then place into an embroidery hoop (see page 12).

1 Start by working the outline of the moon in back stitch using one strand of medium old gold.

2 Fill the moon with tiny flower petals. First, choose a dot in the middle of the moon, and start by making five petals around it using three strands of light old gold to make short seed stitches. Repeat this pattern as many times as you can to cover all the space inside the moon. It's fine to use fewer petals here and there.

3 Spot your flowers and make a French knot in the middle of each of them using two strands of medium old gold. You can also cover the black areas with French knots to create the illusion that there are more flowers.

4 Using three strands of precious metals dark gold, work very small straight stitches to make the tiny dots around the moon.

5

Perfect Patches

LOVER'S EYE

TEMPLATE *Page* 121 REFERENCE

Capture the opulence of the Renaissance period with this arty eye surrounded by a teardrop of pearls.

TOOLS AND MATERIALS

- Transfer and marking tools
- White or tan duck cotton fabric
- Hoop
- Needle
- Scissors
- 4 mm pearls
- Dark-colour felt sheet
- Piece of sponge
- Glue

THREAD COLOURS USED

- Black, 2 strands
- White, 6 strands
- Dark golden olive, 3 strands
- Medium golden olive, 3 strands
- Light tan, 2 strands
- Light hazelnut brown, 2 strands
- Ultra very light terracotta, 3 strands
- Very dark golden olive, 2 strands

STITCHES USED

- Satin stitch
- Straight stitch

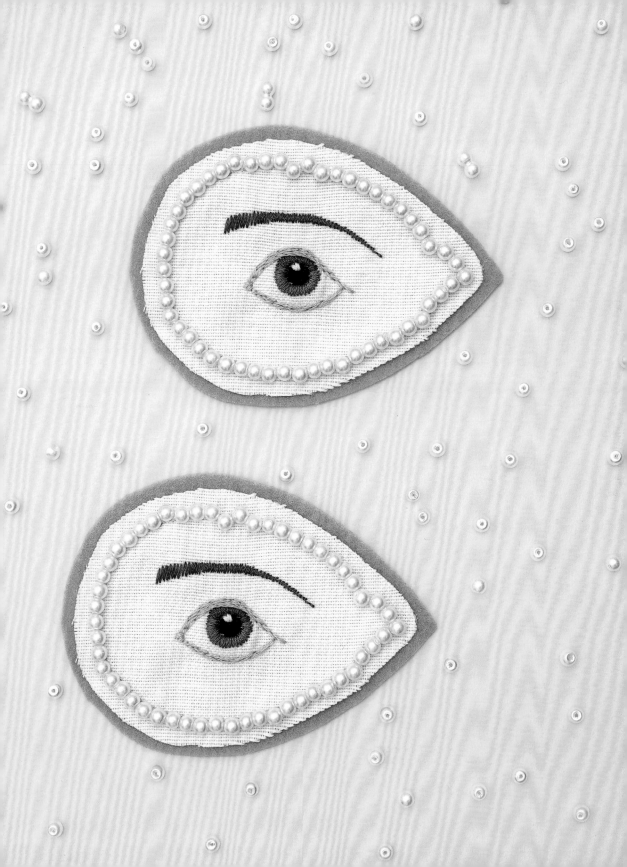

THE PROCESS

Transfer the lover's eye motif (see Templates, page 121, or, alternatively, you can use the iron-on transfer paper at the back of the book) onto the piece of fabric, then place into an embroidery hoop (see page 12).

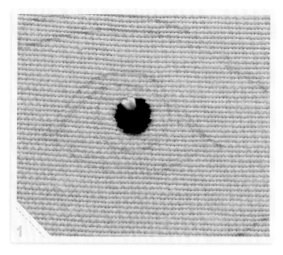

Starting with the pupil of the eye, satin stitch the area using two strands of black. To create the light effect, make tiny little straight stitches on the pupil using six strands of white.

Stitch the top area of the iris in satin stitch using three strands of dark golden olive. Make sure you work your stitches from the edge of the eyelid in towards the pupil.

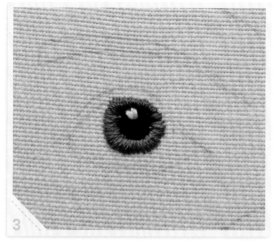

Continue working the bottom part of the iris in satin stitch using three strands of medium golden olive. Work the stitches in the same direction as before, from the edge of the iris in towards the pupil.

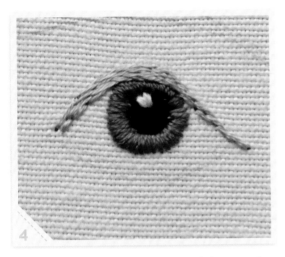

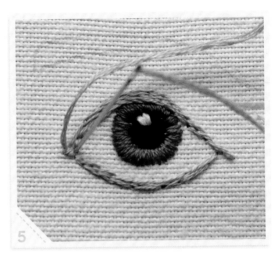

Stitch the top eyelid by working long and short straight stitches in the direction of the eyelid using two strands of light tan. Make sure you follow its bow-like shape.

Stitch the bottom eyelid in the same way as Step 4 but using two strands of light hazelnut brown instead. Using satin stitch and three strands of ultra very light terracotta, fill in the little area where the eyelid starts.

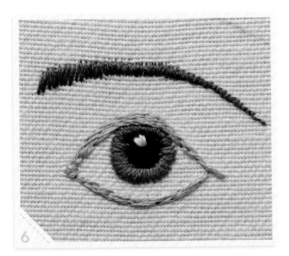

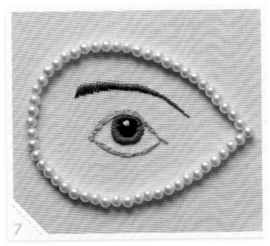

Work the eyebrow in satin stitch using two strands of very dark golden olive. Leave a tiny space between your stitches to create a nice eyebrow texture.

Sew on the pearls, following the outline of the teardrop shape around the eye.

HAND HOLDING FLOWER

TEMPLATE *Page* 120 REFERENCE

Sometimes we all need a helping hand, and this design, featuring the universally recognised symbol of friendship, makes a fantastic embellishment for a variety of projects, from pockets to pendants.

TOOLS AND MATERIALS
- Transfer and marking tools
- White duck cotton fabric
- Hoop
- Needle
- Scissors
- Felt sheet in colour of your choice
- Piece of sponge
- Glue

THREAD COLOURS USED
- Black, 2 strands
- Medium topaz, 6 strands
- Medium brown, 3 strands
- Dark blue green, 6 strands

STITCHES USED
- Split stitch
- Satin stitch
- French knots
- Back stitch

Transfer the hand motif (see Templates, page 120, or, alternatively, you can use the iron-on transfer paper at the back of the book) onto the piece of fabric, then place into an embroidery hoop (see page 12). Work the outline of the hand in split stitch using two strands of black.

The next step is the flower. Starting with the petals, work each of them in satin stitch using six strands of medium topaz.

Fill in the middle of the flower by making a cluster of French knots, using three strands of medium brown. To finish, work the stem of the flower in back stitch using six strands of dark blue green.

CAT PAW

TEMPLATE
Page
121
REFERENCE

Everybody loves a cute kitten, and this adorable cat paw patch makes the perfect gift for cat lovers everywhere. Why not try adding it as a tag on a cat's collar?

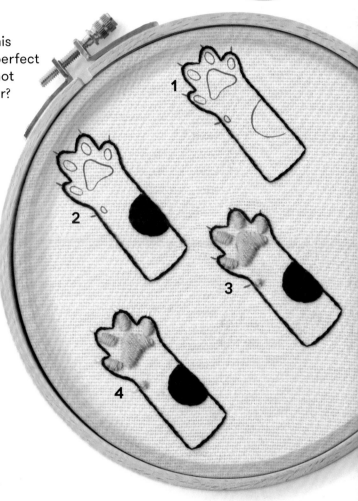

TOOLS AND MATERIALS

- Transfer and marking tools
- White duck cotton fabric
- Hoop
- Needle
- Scissors
- Felt sheet in colour of your choice
- Piece of sponge
- Glue

THREAD COLOURS USED

- Black, 6 strands
- Light coral, 6 strands
- White, 3 strands

STITCHES USED

- Split stitch
- Satin stitch
- Seed stitch

THE PROCESS

Transfer the cat paw motif (see Templates, page 121, or, alternatively, you can use the iron-on transfer paper at the back of the book) onto the piece of fabric, then place into an embroidery hoop (see page 12).

1 Start by making the outline of the paw in split stitch using two strands of black.

2 Work the spot on the paw in split stitch using four strands of black. Work the outline first, and then make smaller loops inside to fill the space.

3 Next, work the pink pads in satin stitch using six strands of light coral. The direction of each toe bean should be as pictured.

4 Cover the nails with three strands of white, and make a single seed stitch for each of them.

FANCY PANSY

TEMPLATE *Page* 125 REFERENCE

You can often find this colourful little flower in bloom throughout the year. Customise the pattern in your own colours to brighten up a favourite sweater or pair of jeans.

TOOLS AND MATERIALS

- Transfer and marking tools
- Duck cotton fabric in colour of your choice
- Hoop
- Needle
- Scissors
- Pearl beads
- Felt sheet in colour of your choice
- Piece of sponge
- Glue

THREAD COLOURS USED

- Ultra very dark turquoise, 6 strands
- Dark navy blue, 6 strands
- Light topaz, 6 strands
- Dark garnet, 6 strands
- Ultra very light terracotta, 6 strands
- Medium topaz, 6 strands

STITCHES USED

- Satin stitch
- Straight stitch

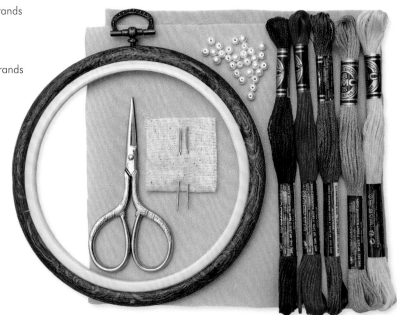

THE PROCESS

Transfer the fancy pansy motif (see Templates, page 125, or, alternatively, you can use the iron-on transfer paper at the back of the book) onto the piece of fabric, then place into an embroidery hoop (see page 12).

Start with the pansy on the top left and, in satin stitch, work all of its petals using six strands of ultra very dark turquoise.

To create the pattern, make long and short straight stitches inside each petal using six strands of dark navy blue. Start your stitches from the centre of the pansy and take them out to any spot near the edge of the petal.

Now work the pansy on the top right in the same way as Step 1, this time using six strands of light topaz.

Use six strands of dark garnet to make the pattern inside the petal, once again using long and short straight stitches, worked from the centre outwards.

Now stitch the pansy on the bottom in exactly the same way as Steps 1 and 2 using six strands of ultra very light terracotta for the petals, and six strands of medium topaz for the pattern inside.

To finish, sew a pearl bead into the middle of each pansy using two strands of any colour thread.

MONSTERA LEAVES

TEMPLATE
Page
119
REFERENCE

The tropical look never goes out of fashion, so why not channel the botanical vibe with this marvellous monstera leaf, guaranteed to always be on trend?

TOOLS AND MATERIALS

- Transfer and marking tools
- Duck cotton fabric in colour of your choice
- Hoop
- Needle
- Scissors
- Mint-green toho beads
- Green sequins
- Felt sheet in colour of your choice
- Piece of sponge
- Glue

THREAD COLOURS USED

- Medium teal green, 4 strands
- Light green, 7 strands
- Very light aquamarine, 3 strands
- Light Nile green, 2 strands
- Chartreuse, 2 strands

STITCHES USED

- Split stitch
- Back stitch
- French knots

THE PROCESS

Transfer the monstera motif (see Templates, page 119, or, alternatively, you can use the iron-on transfer paper at the back of the book) onto the piece of fabric, then place into an embroidery hoop (see page 12).

Starting with the monstera leaf on the left, split stitch its outline using four strands of medium teal green.

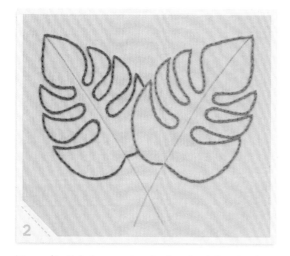

Now split stitch the monstera leaf on the right using four strands of light green.

Work the left leaf's stem in back stitch using three strands of light green. Then do the same for the leaf on the right using three strands of very light aquamarine.

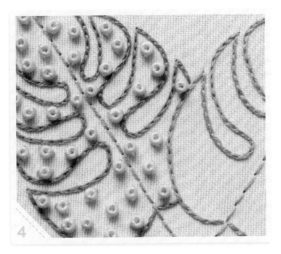

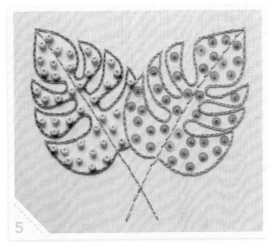

Using two strands of light Nile green, sew the mint toho beads inside the leaf on the left, taking care to leave some space between each bead.

To attach the green sequins inside the leaf on the right, use two strands of chartreuse and work a French knot through the hole in the middle of each sequin.

BIG FISH

TEMPLATE Page 120 REFERENCE

They say life is better down where it's wetter, and if this cheerful-looking fish is anything to go by, they couldn't be more right. Time to grab your swimsuit and take a dip. . .

TOOLS AND MATERIALS

- Transfer and marking tools
- Duck cotton fabric in colour of your choice
- Hoop
- Needle
- Scissors
- 0.8 mm grey or blue toho beads (optional)
- Felt sheet in colour of your choice
- Piece of sponge
- Glue

THREAD COLOURS USED

- Black, 3 strands
- Ecru, 2 strands
- White, 1 strand
- Ultra very light terracotta, 3 strands
- Apricot, 4 strands
- Very light peach, 5 strands
- Tan, 1 strand
- Light tan, 1 strand
- Dark antique blue, 6 strands
- Dark green grey, 6 strands
- Light pewter, 8 strands

STITCHES USED

- Satin stitch
- Split stitch
- Straight stitch
- Stem stitch
- Brick stitch

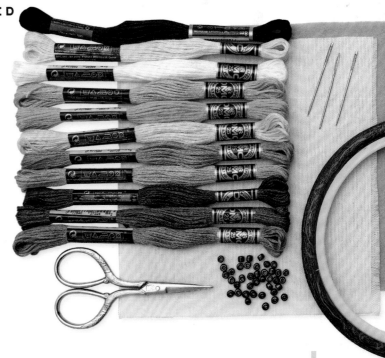

THE PROCESS

Transfer the fish motif (see Templates, page 120, or, alternatively, you can use the iron-on transfer paper at the back of the book) onto the piece of fabric, then place into an embroidery hoop (see page 12).

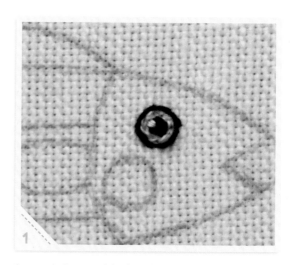

Start with the eye of the fish, first working the pupil in satin stitch using two strands of black. Next, use split stitch and two strands of ecru to work a loop around the pupil. Once you have finished your loop, make a tiny straight stitch on the pupil using one strand of white, to create the light effect. Finally, outline the pewter area in stem stitch, using one strand of black.

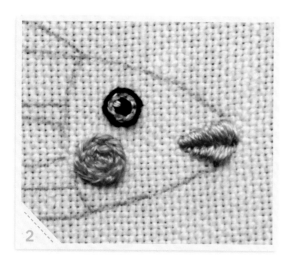

Work the lips in satin stitch using three strands of ultra very light terracotta. Now fill in the cheek with split stitch using four strands of apricot. Start with the outer edge, then work smaller, decreasing loops into the centre.

Outline the head with split stitch using two strands of very light peach. Then fill the inside by working small straight stitches in different directions, this time using three strands of very light peach.

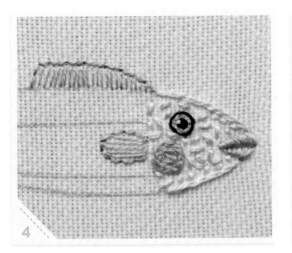

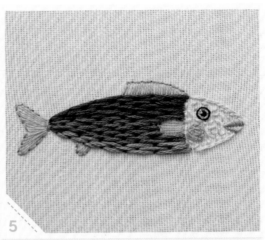

Work the outlines of the fins and the tail in stem stitch using one strand of tan. To fill them, work straight stitch inside each area using one strand of light tan. Leave a little space between your straight stitches to create a nice fish tail and fin pattern.

Fill in the upper part of the body with brick stitch using six strands of dark antique blue. Continue to work the rest of the body in brick stitch, using six strands of dark green grey for the middle part, and six strands of light pewter for the lower part.

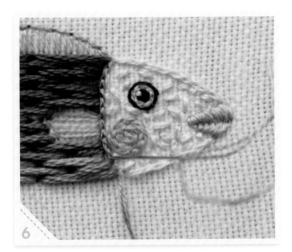

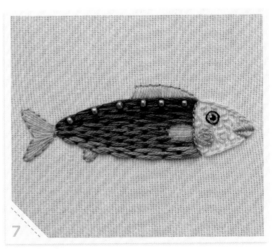

Make the line between the face and the body (near the cheek) in split stitch using two strands of light pewter.

Finish by sewing some toho beads to the upper part of the body to embellish your patch (optional).

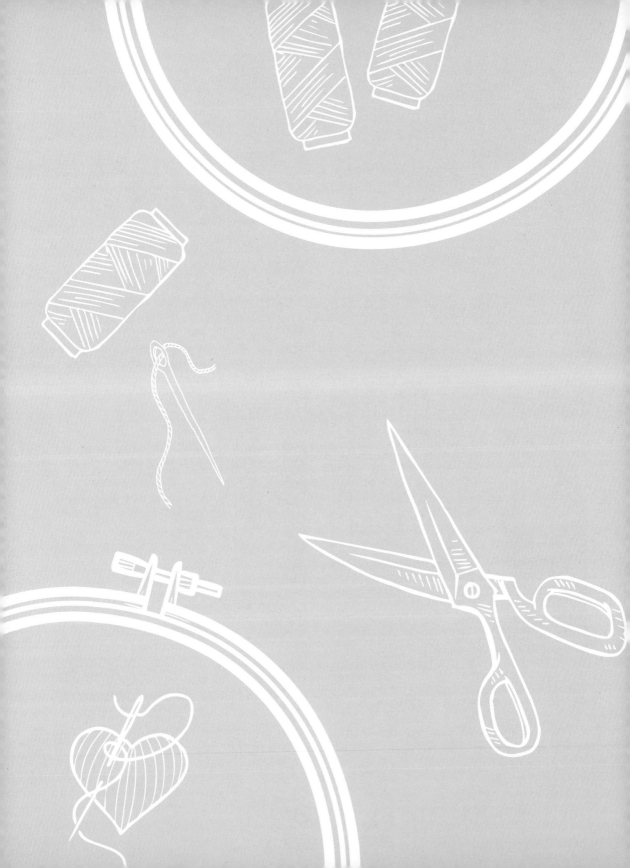

6

Brilliant Badges

TREE HUGGER

It is a scientifically proven fact that hugging a tree makes you feel better, so show some love for our planet with this cute badge.

TEMPLATE
REFERENCE
Page
119

TOOLS AND MATERIALS

- Transfer and marking tools
- Duck cotton fabric in colour of your choice
- Hoop
- Needle
- Scissors
- Felt sheet in colour of your choice

THREAD COLOURS USED

- Tawny, 2 strands
- Very dark hazelnut brown, 4 strands
- Dark hazelnut brown, 1 strand
- Medium jade, 6 strands
- Medium light moss green, 2 strands

STITCHES USED

- Satin stitch
- Split stitch
- Back stitch
- Straight stitch

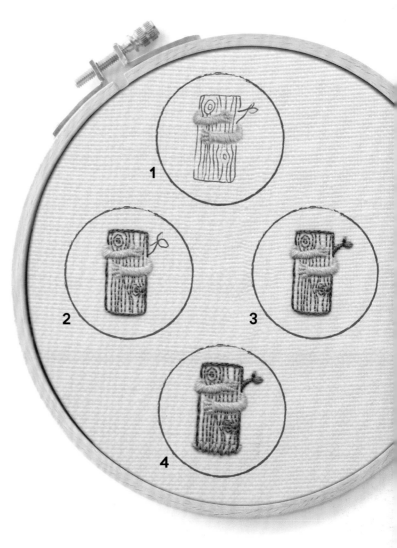

THE PROCESS

Transfer the tree hugger motif (see Templates, page 119, or, alternatively, you can use the iron-on transfer paper at the back of the book) onto the piece of fabric, then place into an embroidery hoop (see page 12).

1 Start by working both of the arms in satin stitch using two strands of tawny. Then narrow your stitches and make each finger in satin stitch, too.

2 For the tree, begin by working its outline in split stitch using two strands of very dark hazelnut brown. Then work the wood pattern in back stitch using one strand of dark hazelnut brown.

3 To make the little branch on the right, use satin stitch and two strands of very dark hazelnut brown. Then work the leaves in straight stitch using six strands of medium jade.

4 Finally, add some grass under the tree by working a series of V-shaped straight stitches using two strands of medium light moss green.

STARGAZER

TEMPLATE
Page
123
REFERENCE

Guess the constellation and get starry-eyed over this on-trend tribute to astronomy, which also makes a great pendant or a cute addition to a shirt collar.

TOOLS AND MATERIALS

- Transfer and marking tools
- Black or deep-blue duck cotton fabric
- Hoop
- Needle
- Scissors
- Felt sheet in colour of your choice

THREAD COLOURS USED

- White, 6 strands
- Very light old gold, 1 strand

STITCHES USED

- Back stitch
- French knots
- Straight stitch

THE PROCESS

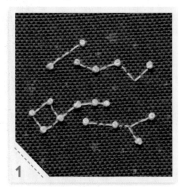

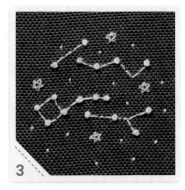

Transfer the stargazer motif (see Templates, page 123, or, alternatively, you can use the iron-on transfer paper at the back of the book) onto the piece of fabric, then place into an embroidery hoop (see page 12). To begin, work all of the connection lines in back stitch using one strand of white. Next, stitch the dots on the connection lines by making French knots with two strands of white.

Make the stars by working their outlines in straight stitch using one strand of very light old gold. Stitch them as if you were drawing a star on paper.

Finally, work the tiny surrounding dots in straight stitch using three strands of white.

EMBROIDERY ENTHUSIAST

What better way to celebrate your love of embroidery than by stitching this super-cute badge? Pin it proudly to your jacket or bag and display your crafting skills for all the world to see.

TOOLS AND MATERIALS
- Transfer and marking tools
- Duck cotton fabric in colour of your choice
- Hoop
- Needle
- Scissors
- Felt sheet in colour of your choice

THREAD COLOURS USED
- Precious metal effects silver, 3 strands
- Bright red, 5 strands
- Medium grey blue, 1 strand

STITCHES USED
- Back stitch
- Split stitch
- Seed stitch

THE PROCESS

Transfer the embroidery enthusiast motif (see Templates, page 120, or, alternatively, you can use the iron-on transfer paper at the back of the book) onto the piece of fabric, then place into an embroidery hoop (see page 12).

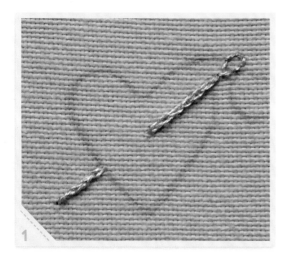

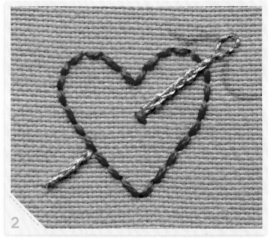

Start by working the eye of the needle in back stitch using one strand of precious metal effects silver. Next, stitch the body of the needle in split stitch using two strands of precious metal effects silver.

Work the outline of the heart in back stitch using three strands of bright red.

Work the piece of thread in back stitch using one strand of medium grey blue.

Finally, fill the inside of the heart with seed stitch using two strands of bright red.

MORNING SURVIVOR

TEMPLATE *Page* REFERENCE 119

We all know that feeling when it's just too much of a struggle to get up and moving in the morning, but sometimes all we need is a cup of coffee to make it better. Celebrate your victory over another early start, and salute the humble coffee bean with this cute badge.

TOOLS AND MATERIALS

- Transfer and marking tools
- Duck cotton fabric in colour of your choice
- Hoop
- Needle
- Scissors
- Felt sheet in colour of your choice

THREAD COLOURS USED

- Apricot, 2 strands
- Dark mocha brown, 3 strands
- Medium topaz, 9 strands
- Light aquamarine, 2 strands
- Medium apricot, 1 strand
- Light jade, 3 strands
- Very light old gold, 1 strand

STITCHES USED

- Satin stitch
- Straight stitch
- Split stitch
- Seed stitch
- Back stitch

THE PROCESS

Transfer the morning survivor motif (see Templates, page 119, or, alternatively, you can use the iron-on transfer paper at the back of the book) onto the piece of fabric, then place into an embroidery hoop (see page 12).

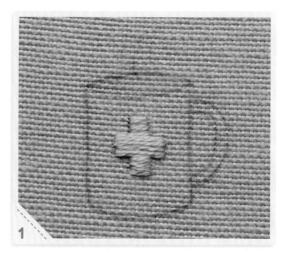

Start with the first aid icon on the coffee mug, working it in satin stitch using two strands of apricot.

To create the coffee inside the mug, make horizontal, freestyle long and short straight stitches using three strands of dark mocha brown.

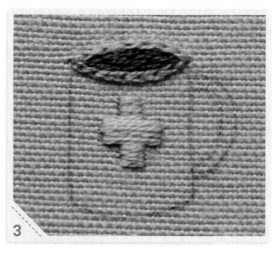

Outline the rim of the mug in split stitch using three strands of medium topaz.

Outline the edges of the mug in split stitch using two strands of light aquamarine.

Work the handle of the mug in split stitch using six strands of medium topaz, making sure you start your loop in the middle of the mug outline. Outline the edges of the first aid icon in straight stitch using one strand of medium apricot.

Fill the mug background with tiny seed stitches using three strands of light jade.

To finish, outline the tendrils of steam in back stitch using one strand of very light old gold.

7

Stitch Directory

STITCH DIRECTORY

This chapter illustrates how to form all of the stitches used to create the projects in the book. Each stitch is clearly explained with step-by-step instructions and helpful diagrams, with finished examples of the stitch to show how it can be applied.

STRAIGHT STITCH

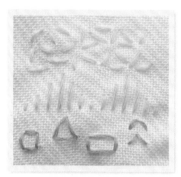

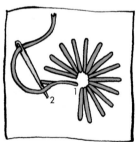

Bring the needle up at 1 and then insert it at 2. Repeat as required.

Note
Straight stitches of similar lengths placed close together at random angles are also referred to as 'seed stitch'.

SATIN STITCH

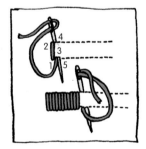

Bring the needle up at 1, down at 2, up at 3, down at 4 and up at 5. Repeat as required. The stitches should be close together, with no fabric showing between them.

Note
For a more defined and slightly raised edge, first outline the shape with split stitch or stem stitch, then satin stitch as described above, just over the stitched outline.

BACK STITCH

Bring the needle up at 1, down at 2 and up at 3. The distance of 1–2 should be the same as the distance of 1–3. Begin the next stitch by inserting the needle at 1 again. Repeat as required, keeping the stitch length constant.

BRICK STITCH

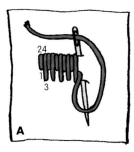

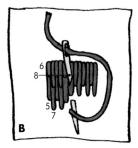

A   **B**

Fig. A
Begin stitching along the outline with a row of long and short stitches: bring the needle up at 1, down at 2, up at 3 and down at 4. Repeat.

Fig. B
For the second row, bring the needle up at 5, down at 6, piercing the base of the short stitch above, up at 7 and down at 8, piercing the base of the long stitch above. Repeat. Note that the stitches in the second and all subsequent rows should be the same length; only the first and last rows will actually use a combination of long and short stitches. End with a row of long and short stitches.

FRENCH KNOTS

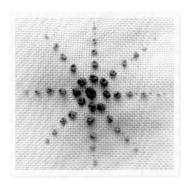

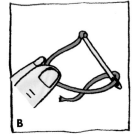

A   **B**

Fig. A
Bring the needle up at 1. Holding the thread taut with the finger and thumb of your other hand, tightly wind the thread twice around the tip of the needle.

Fig. B
Still holding the thread, insert the needle very close to 1 and pull it through to the back of the work so the twists are lying neatly on the surface of the fabric. Repeat as required.

Note
For a smaller French knot, wrap the thread around the needle just once in Fig. A. For a larger knot, wrap the thread three or four times.

SPLIT STITCH

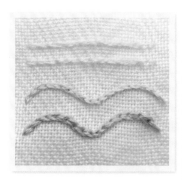

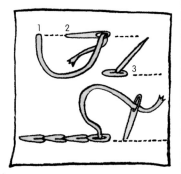

Bring the needle up at 1 and down at 2. Pull the thread through firmly. Bring the needle up again at 3, through the centre of the previous stitch. Repeat as required.

STEM STITCH

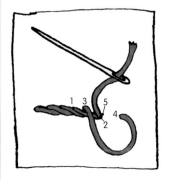

Bring the needle up at 1, down at 2 and up at 3, halfway between 1 and 2, above the stitch. Bring the needle down at 4 and up next to 2 (at 5), above the stitch. Repeat to the end of the line. Each stitch should be the same length, and begin halfway along the previous stitch.

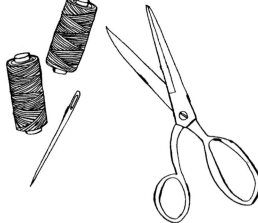

ADDING SEQUINS AND BEADS

HOW TO SEW A SEQUIN

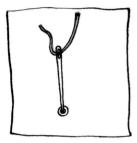  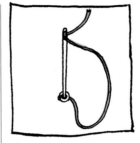 

1 Use a needle that is thinner than the hole of your sequin. Identify the place where you'll sew your sequin, and bring the needle up through the fabric. Draw it through the centre of the sequin.

2 Insert your needle close to the edge of your sequin and pull out to the back of the fabric again.

3 Repeat this one more time by inserting your needle to another point of the edge to make it durable.

HOW TO SEW A BEAD

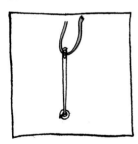 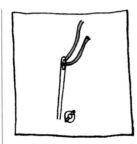 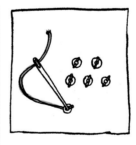 

1 Thread a very fine tapestry or beading needle with 1 ply of DMC Mouline. You can use the same colour as your bead or experiment with different colours. Identify the place where you'll sew your bead, and bring up your needle at that point. Thread your bead through the needle.

2 Insert your needle quite close to your initial entry point and pull out to the back of the fabric again.

3 Repeat the same stitching until you have made sure that it's durable.

Transfers and Templates

TRANSFERRING THE DESIGN

To use a motif exactly as it appears in the Templates at the back of the book, just trace it onto a sheet of tracing paper and transfer the design to your piece of fabric.

STENCIL METHOD

This method is useful for transferring designs to ready-made garments, and it is ideal for creating repeating patterns. This method works best with bold shapes that don't have a lot of detail.

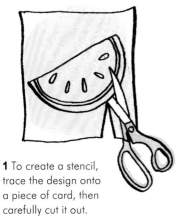

1 To create a stencil, trace the design onto a piece of card, then carefully cut it out.

2 Place the card stencil on top of the piece of fabric and draw around the edge, filling in any details by hand if necessary.

TO ENLARGE OR REDUCE A MOTIF

Use a photocopier and specify the percentage by which you need to enlarge or reduce the motif.

$$\frac{\text{Desired size}}{\text{Existing size}} \times 100 =$$

approximate percentage to enlarge or reduce the pattern

TRACING PAPER

Place a sheet of tracing paper over the motif and trace the design with a pencil. Remove the tracing paper and, if necessary, darken the traced lines by going over them with a finetip marker or pen. Choose whichever transfer method you like.

FREEZER PAPER METHOD

 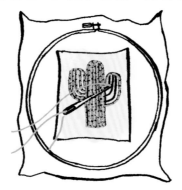 

1 Use a regular pen or pencil to trace the design onto the non-shiny side of a piece of freezer paper.

2 Place the freezer paper on top of the piece of fabric, with the shiny side facing down, and then use a warm iron to temporarily stick the freezer paper to the fabric. You can then stitch directly over it.

3 Once your embroidery work is complete, use tweezers to gently tear away the paper in small pieces, making sure you don't pull on the stitches. This method works well with materials like dark-coloured felt that are tricky to mark with a pen or pencil.

TRACING WITH A LIGHT SOURCE

Direct tracing using a light box is probably the simplest way to transfer a design to a piece of fabric. Place the design on top of the light box, with the right side facing up, so that the design is lit from beneath. Place the piece of fabric on top of the design and position as necessary. Trace the lines of the design with the marking tool most suitable for the type of fabric you're using.

WATER-SOLUBLE STABILISER

Designs can be traced with a pencil or printed directly onto a piece of water-soluble film or paper, which also acts as a fabric stabiliser. Pin or tack the piece of film/paper to the right side of the fabric and embroider over it. Alternatively, you can use a hoop to hold the film/paper in position against the piece of fabric. Once you've finished embroidering, rinse the fabric in water, following the manufacturer's instructions, to remove all traces of the stabiliser.

IRON-ON PATTERN SHEETS

1 Pin the piece of fabric to a slightly padded surface. Pin the iron-on pattern sheet in place, with the ink side facing down. The design will be reversed. Use a hot iron to press down on the sheet for about 30 seconds. Do not slide the iron, but lift and replace it to cover the whole design.

2 Carefully lift one corner of the iron-on pattern sheet to see if the design has fully transferred. If not, apply more heat until all the design lines have transferred cleanly. Bear in mind that transferred lines are normally permanent and will have to be completely covered with stitches later.

CARBON PAPER

Dressmaker's carbon paper works in the same way as ordinary carbon paper, but it is made specifically for fabric. Place the piece of fabric on a flat surface, with the right side facing up. Place the design to be traced on top of the fabric. Tuck a sheet of dressmaker's carbon paper between the fabric and the design, with the carbon side facing the fabric. Carefully trace over the design with a pencil or stylus.

TEMPLATES

Feel free to mix and match the templates featured here. This basic formula will help you resize your motif so it works as a button, badge, pin, patch or tiny hoop.

$$\frac{\text{Desired size}}{\text{Existing size}} \times 100 = \begin{array}{c} \text{approximate} \\ \text{percentage to} \\ \text{enlarge or reduce} \\ \text{the pattern} \end{array}$$

TINY HOOP

← 8 cm (3 in) →

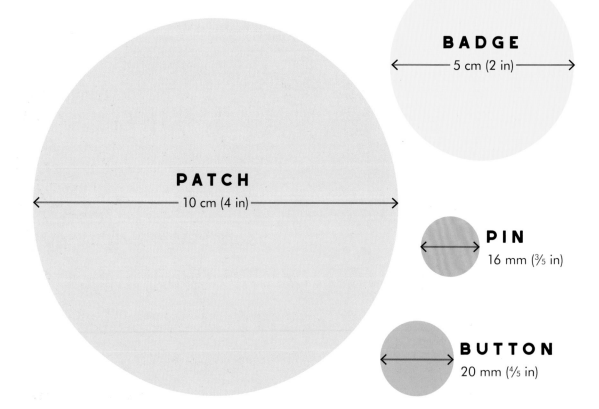

BADGE

← 5 cm (2 in) →

PATCH

← 10 cm (4 in) →

PIN

16 mm (³⁄₅ in)

BUTTON

20 mm (⁴⁄₅ in)

SUMMER SUNSET: P30

TREE HUGGER: P96

PINEAPPLE PARADISE: P38

PLANET SATURN: P50

POPPY: P46

THE BEE'S KNEES: P40

MORNING SURVIVOR: P104

MONSTERA LEAVES: P86

EMBROIDERY ENTHUSIAST: P100

ICE-CREAM CONE: P66

LIKE A MOTH TO A FLAME: P60

HAND HOLDING FLOWER: P78

BIG FISH: P90

LOVER'S EYE: P74

ROCKIN' ROBIN: P42

CAT PAW: P80

A NIGHT IN THE FOREST: P20

DESERT LANDCAPE: P24

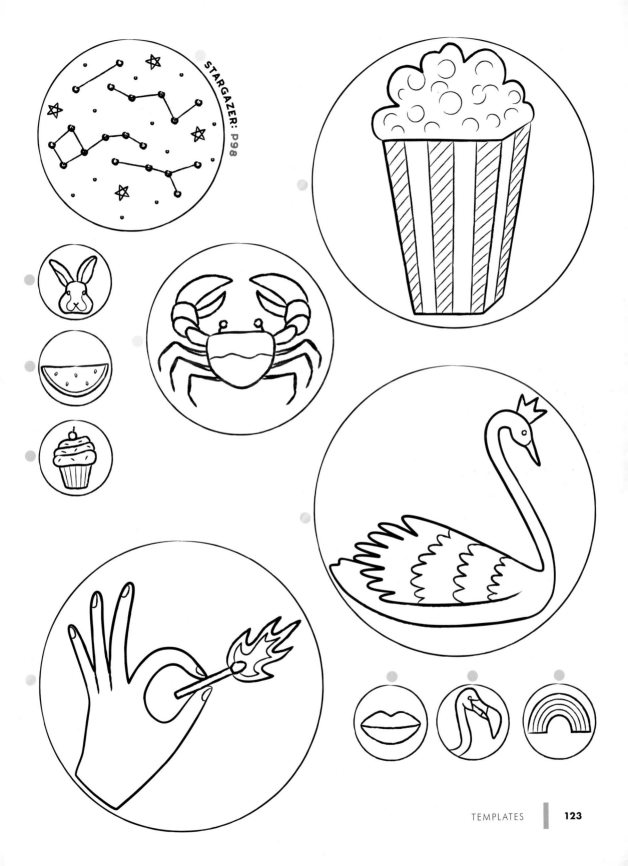

STARGAZER: P98

OVER THE FLORAL MOON: P70

THE ALL-SEEING EYE: P56

PRICKLY CACTUS: P64

INDEX

Illustrations are in italics, **projects** **in bold.**

THREADS USED

I have used DMC threads for the projects in this book, but you can use any cotton embroidery thread.

A NIGHT IN THE FOREST
DMC 563 – Light jade
DMC 3816 – Celadon green
DMC 501 – Dark blue green
DMC 732 – Olive green
DMC 733 – Medium olive green
DMC 3341 – Apricot
DMC 3822 – Light straw
DMC 435 – Light brown
DMC 3013 – Light khaki green
DMC 3047 – Light yellow beige
DMC E3852 – Precious metals dark gold

DESERT LANDSCAPE
DMC 501 – Dark blue green
DMC 3816 – Celadon green
DMC 563 – Light jade
DMC 3607 – Light plum
DMC 680 – Dark old gold
DMC 730 – Very dark olive green
DMC 831 – Medium golden olive
DMC 833 – Light golden olive
DMC 166 – Medium light moss green
DMC 210 – Medium lavender
DMC 955 – Light Nile green
DMC 436 – Tan
DMC 729 – Medium gold
DMC 3772 – Very dark desert sand
DMC 3064 – Desert sand
DMC 3771 – Ultra very light terracotta
DMC 445 – Light lemon
DMC 562 – Medium jade
DMC 3340 – Medium apricot
DMC 3341 – Apricot

SUMMER SUNSET
DMC 3809 – Very dark turquoise
DMC 954 – Nile green
DMC 3689 – Light mauve
DMC 3340 – Medium apricot
DMC 606 – Bright orange red
DMC 676 – Light old gold
DMC 3829 – Very dark old gold
DMC 645 – Very dark beaver grey
DMC White
DMC 926 – Medium green grey
DMC 3768 – Dark green grey
DMC 930 – Dark antique blue

DMC 3341 – Apricot
DMC 3047 – Light yellow beige
DMC 831 – Medium golden olive

PINEAPPLE PARADISE
DMC 3821 – Medium mustard
DMC 435 – Light brown
DMC 561 – Very dark jade
DMC 562 – Medium jade

THE BEE'S KNEES
DMC 844 – Ultra dark beaver grey
DMC 728 – Topaz
DMC 3047 – Light yellow beige

ROCKIN' ROBIN
DMC 722 – Light orange spice
DMC 3032 – Medium mocha brown
DMC 611 – Drab brown
DMC 3866 – Mocha brown
DMC Ecru
DMC 310 – Black
DMC 844 – Ultra dark beaver grey
DMC 830 – Dark golden olive

POPPY
DMC 606 – Bright orange red
DMC 608 – Bright orange
DMC 3340 – Medium apricot
DMC 831 – Medium golden olive
DMC 832 – Golden olive
DMC 3787 – Dark brown grey
DMC 782 – Dark topaz
DMC White

PLANET SATURN
DMC 3825 – Pale pumpkin
DMC 3607 – Light plum
DMC E3852 – Precious metals dark gold

THE ALL-SEEING EYE
DMC 680 – Dark gold
DMC 833 – Light golden olive
DMC 435 – Light brown
DMC 310 – Black
DMC White
DMC 3340 – Medium apricot
DMC 3341 – Apricot
DMC E3852 – Precious metals dark gold

LIKE A MOTH TO A FLAME
DMC 829 – Very dark golden olive
DMC 3341 – Apricot
DMC 967 – Very light apricot
DMC 563 – Light jade
DMC 734 – Light olive green
DMC 445 – Light lemon
DMC 310 – Black

PRICKLY CACTUS
DMC 3816 – Celadon green
DMC 3822 – Light straw
DMC 3340 – Medium apricot
DMC 782 – Dark topaz

ICE-CREAM CONE
DMC 3822 – Light straw
DMC 964 – Light sea green
DMC 3341 – Apricot
DMC 729 – Medium gold
DMC 435 – Light brown
DMC 955 – Light Nile green

OVER THE FLORAL MOON
DMC 729 – Medium old gold
DMC 676 – Light old gold
DMC E3852 – Precious metals dark gold

LOVER'S EYE
DMC 3771 – Ultra very light terracotta
DMC 310 – Black
DMC White
DMC 437 – Light tan
DMC 422 – Light hazelnut brown
DMC 830 – Dark golden olive
DMC 831 – Medium golden olive
DMC 829 – Very dark golden olive

HAND HOLDING FLOWER
DMC 310 – Black
DMC 783 – Medium topaz
DMC 433 – Medium Brown
DMC 501 – Dark blue green

CAT PAW
DMC 310 – Black
DMC 352 – Light coral
DMC White

FANCY PANSY
DMC 3808 – Ultra very dark turquoise

DMC 823 – Dark navy blue
DMC 726 – Light topaz
DMC 814 – Dark garnet
DMC 3779 – Ultra very light terracotta
DMC 783 – Medium topaz

MONSTERA LEAVES
DMC 3848 – Medium teal green
DMC 3851 – Light green
DMC 703 – Chartreuse
DMC 993 – Very light aquamarine
DMC 955 – Light Nile green

BIG FISH
DMC 310 – Black
DMC Ecru
DMC White
DMC 3771 – Ultra very light terracotta
DMC 3341 – Apricot
DMC 948 – Very light peach
DMC 436 – Tan
DMC 437 – Light tan
DMC 930 – Dark antique blue
DMC 3768 – Dark green grey
DMC 169 – Light pewter

TREE HUGGER
DMC 945 – Tawny
DMC 869 – Very dark hazelnut brown
DMC 420 – Dark hazelnut brown
DMC 562 – Medium jade
DMC 166 – Medium light moss green

STARGAZER
DMC White
DMC 677 – Very light old gold

EMBROIDERY ENTHUSIAST
DMC E168 5283 – Precious metal effects silver
DMC 666 – Bright red
DMC 160 – Medium grey blue

MORNING SURVIVOR
DMC 3341 – Apricot
DMC 3781 – Dark mocha brown
DMC 783 – Medium topaz
DMC 992 – Light aquamarine
DMC 563 – Light jade
DMC 3340 – Medium apricot
DMC 677 – Very light old gold